I0198484

The **ABC**s
of a **TROUBLED REPUBLIC**

The **ABC**s
of a **TROUBLED REPUBLIC**

Musings on American Values

MEG GORZYCKI

RESOURCE *Publications* • Eugene, Oregon

THE ABCS OF A TROUBLED REPUBLIC
Musings on American Values

Resource Publications
An Imprint of Wipf and Stock Publishers
199 W. 8th Ave., Suite 3
Eugene, OR 97401

www.wipfandstock.com

PAPERBACK ISBN: 978-1-5326-9968-9
HARDCOVER ISBN: 978-1-5326-9969-6
EBOOK ISBN: 978-1-5326-9970-2

10/08/19

Introduction

Here's a little book,
I keep beside my bed,
It helps me remember,
What the Gospel said.

It might be quirky,
A naughty little book;
But the way we are living,
Needs a second look.

A Is for adversaries,
Who won't cross the aisle,
They don't say "hello"
They won't even smile.

Absolutely abhorrent,
They are a disgrace;
Democracy's dialogue
All up in our face.

See Jack hit Timmy.
What could it be?
Jack hit Timmy
'Cuz they don't agree.

B Is for budget,
It's messy, you bet,
Most of it goes
To service the debt.

Balancing bounty
Can be just the worst;
When parties insist
Special interests come first.

See Bobby brag.
"Look what I got!"
"I got the public
To pay for my yacht!"

C Is for crashing,
At age sixty-two,
When life-long employers
Want nothing from you.

The boss wants cheap labor,
Not the wisdom you hold;
So out with the garbage,
We go 'cuz we're old!"

Hear Mike's boss.
"Retire, Mike retire!"
Mike wants to work.
Fire him, fire!

D Is for distractions,
We have quite a few,
Like texting and TV,
And Internet too.

We're buzzing and beeping
And look for the thrill;
Imagine the sanity,
If we could sit still!

Cathy takes a selfie,
She is such a dear.
Everywhere she goes,
She's looking for a mirror.

E Is for entitlement,
It goes left and right;
It robs us of justice
And makes us uptight.

It conjures excuses
For lopsided wealth,
And depletes the soul
Of our spiritual health.

Jane wants candy.

Now! Now! Now!

Mickey's in the way.

Plow! Plow! Plow!

F Is for factious,
When egos collide,
The stubborn take solace
By taking a side.

In corners we stew
Not much to discuss;
We don't like them,
And they don't like us.

See Dick snub Sally.
He thinks he's right.
Snub! Snub! Snub!
Oh! What a fight!

G Is for greatness,
We hope to achieve,
With rule of the people
We still believe.

It's a way of respecting,
A clear way of seeing,
That each is no object,
But a true human being.

Dick is counting.
One! Two! Three!
Dot is barking.
"Don't forget me!"

H Is for homeland,
We cherish so dear,
Protect it, defend it
Wave banners and cheer.

Millions without shelter,
So many unseen;
Millions impoverished,
What does homeland mean?

See grandma move!
She's had seven leases.
No rent control,
Just rent increases!

I Is for imperious,
Not a good way to lead,
It bullies and badgers,
And imposes its creed.

Impatient and impudent
Insisting and vain;
It speeds up the end
Of democracy's reign.

Marco is the master.
Boss! Boss! Boss!
See Jen leave.
It's Marco's loss!

Is for justice,
Elusive and thin,
When suspects are profiled
By color of skin.

When poverty surges
Our civility fails;
We demonize victims
And fill up our jails.

See Scott's house.
Wholesome and pure.
Scott is going to college.
That's for sure!

K Is for kindergarten,
Where we learn the rules,
Then proceed through grades
In poor public schools.

Where politics meddle
That all must advance;
Too much education
Is happening by chance.

See Dick and Jane.
Test! Test! Test!
Hire private tutors
To score the best!

Is for lobbyist,
Their numbers do bloat,
Who carry more weight
Than people who vote.

Insurance firms here
Pharmaceuticals there;
They write legislation
So people. . .BEWARE!

Let's play Washington!
Wheel! Wheel! Wheel!
You play the senator
And I'll make the deal!

M Is for manipulate,
Like splicing DNA,
Making plants grow seedless
To make farmers pay.

What nature once supplied
Is now in corporate hands;
And if we want to eat
We pay up their demands.

See Peg's garden.
All in a row.
See Peg's experiment
Grow! Grow! Grow!

N Is for nonsense,
When people declare,
All liberals are socialists
Pretending to care.

If subsidies signal
An alliance with Marx;
Stop bailing our banks
And rich oligarchs.

Jane doesn't like Susie.
This is what she said:
"Your mommy's a commie!
Red! Red! Red!

Is for oval,
An office revered,
That once stood for virtue
And was not to be feared.

Come scandal, corruption
And threats so unfair;
It's hard to teach children
To respect leaders there.

See Ken thinking.
"Why? Why? Why?
When leaders break the rules,
Why can't I?"

P Is for prayers,
We pray when it's tough,
When working two jobs
Is still not enough.

Hail Mary health care
We're down on our knees;
So we don't lose our homes
Paying hospital fees.

See Father praying.
His prayers are true.
"Lord forget impeachment,
An exorcist will due."

Q Is for quandary,
And wrestle we must,
When we go to the ballot
Who can we trust?

A suit from the left
A brute from the right;
Both keeping agendas
Far from our sight.

Jane heard the candidate.
Bidding, bidding, bidding.
Jane said to mother
"You've got to be kidding!"

R Is for reporter,
Who censors and spins,
Who nails the prophetic
And dotes on who wins.

Officials are nervous
When he comes to call;
If not for elections
They might not talk at all.

Jane told mother a lie.
She said it was a prank.
Mother said, "Not funny!"
Spank! Spank! Spank!

S Is for sinners,
   We thought we once were,
   Before we made fortunes
   And now we're not sure.

   We govern by investments
   And back them with our tanks;
   God can have His heaven
   If we can keep the banks.

Dick sells lemonade.
The mark-up is bad.
Soon he'll be rich.
What a good lad!

Is for temptation,
The urge that we feel,
To exploit our neighbor
To lie, cheat, and steal.

The remedies for temptation
Adjust our attitude;
Be gracious every minute,
With thoughts of gratitude.

Little Sally's neighbors
Have a farm like a zoo.
Whenever she visits,
She talks bar-b-q!

U Is for undertakers,
Who tend to our kids,
When crazed angry shooters
Are flipping their lids.

The collateral damage
Our special cherished ones;
Are the price that we pay
For the love of our guns.

See Dick play.
He plays with the gang.
The gang likes pistols.
Bang! Bang! Bang!

V Is for virtue,
Let's serve up a slice,
We can be generous
Patient, and nice.

Let's be responsible
And clean up our mess;
We can do much better
To relieve our world's stress.

Dot needs a toilet!
Poop! Poop! Poop!
Sally is helpful.
Scoop! Scoop! Scoop!

W Is for weapons,
We invent to win,
They dismember our bodies
And burn up our skin.

Not all innovation
Has honorable merit;
If we blow up the Earth,
What is left to inherit?

See the investor.
He buys much stock.
When wars break out,
His profits will rock!

X Is for xenophobes,
The crouching fearful sorts,
Angry at immigrants
Who land in our ports.

They like low-wage labor
And some scapegoats to blame;
But conveniently forget
From where their families came.

See Dick's bricks.
Stack! Stack! Stack!
Just to be sure
The neighbors don't attack!

Y Is for yearning,
The want that is deep,
It lingers in silence
Which wakens our sleep.

It's bigger than houses
And bright as the sun;
Could it be solace
In knowing we're one?

"Look! Timmy look!
Look and see!
Your exclusive God
Is smiling at me!"

Z Is for zealous,
A trait that goes bad,
When people force others
It makes us all mad.

Zeal can appeal
If what we control,
Is our personal virtue
And the health of our soul.

Poor Sally faltered.
Cry! Cry! Cry!
See mother comfort.
"Try! Try! Try!"

www.ingramcontent.com/pod-product-compliance
Lightning Source LLC
Chambersburg PA
CBHW071400160426
42812CB00085B/723